# PLAY-Engage with Life

DIVYA RAMACHANDRAN

Copyright © 2025 by Divya Ramachandran

All rights reserved.

This book or any portion thereof may not be reproduced or used in any manner whatsoever without the express written permission of the respective author of the respective story, except for the use of brief quotations in a book review.

The writer of the respective work holds sole responsibility for the originality of the content and IndiePress is not responsible in any way whatsoever.

Printed in India

IndiePress

ISBN: 978-93-7197-438-7

First Printing, 2025

IndiePress

A division of Nasadiya Technologies Private Ltd.

Koramangala, Bengaluru

Karnataka-560029

http://indiepress.in/

Edited by Sriya MS

Typeset by MAP Systems, Bengaluru

Book Cover designed by Nikhil Kamath

Publishing Consultant: Bulbul Brahma

# Dedication

*To my puppy, Bella, who watched intently as I wrote every word, sitting right next to me on the sofa, bringing joy, curiosity and endless playfulness to my days.*

# About the Author

Divya Ramachandran is a storyteller, musician, artist and lifelong explorer of creativity and connection. With over 15 years of experience weaving words, melodies and colours, she has built a life full of curiosity, community and play.

Before fully embracing her creative path, Divya earned a Master's in Design Thinking from Milan, Italy and later a Doctorate focused on enhancing classroom experiences through playful augmented reality (AR) technology. Her research combined innovation and imagination to make learning more engaging and joyful—an approach that continues to inspire how she brings creativity into every part of life.

After stepping away from the corporate world of Ed Tech and content creation, Divya dove deep into her passions, learning to live intentionally. This led to the start of the *Happy Wall Community Project*, a mission to splash the city of Bangalore with colours, graffiti and art.

She is also the founder of *Magic Ink*, a storytelling platform for kids where imagination comes alive through stories, audiobooks and playful learning. Divya's books range from children's tales such as *Kitchen Khichdi*, *Yoga with Mr. Foxx*, *Meera and the Magic Kolam* and *Remember Me*, to explorations of creativity and design thinking with *Think Build Create*. Through her stories and projects, she encourages young minds to dream big and build boldly.

***Play: Engage With Life*** is a sequel to her last book, *Think Build Create* and reflects her ongoing journey of creativity, designed for readers ready to embrace their full, vibrant selves—messy, multidimensional and unapologetically alive.

When she's not writing or making music, Divya enjoys hosting gatherings, dancing and dreaming up new adventures to share.

# Author's Note

In today's world, anxiety and depression are rising quietly but steadily, touching more lives than ever before. Despite being more "connected" through social media and technology, many of us feel increasingly alone, overwhelmed and disconnected—caught in a cycle of pressure, comparison and exhaustion. It's easy to lose sight of the simple joys that bring us back to ourselves, the moments that make us feel truly alive.

This book is an invitation to rediscover one such joy: *play*. Not just as a pastime or frivolous activity, but as a powerful, healing practice—a way to reclaim presence, creativity and connection amid life's noise. Through playful exploration, we can soften the weight of anxiety, open ourselves to curiosity and find a path back to joy.

Play is for anyone who has ever felt stuck, unseen, or overwhelmed. It is for those longing to reconnect with their inner child, their creative spark and the world around them. This is a journey of remembering that life is meant to be experienced fully—with wonder, laughter and lightness.

Welcome to the journey. *Let's play!*

— Divya Ramachandran

# Let's Play!

Hey there!

If you're holding this book, chances are you're craving something different—a fresh way to live that's not about hustle culture, perfection, or endless doing.

I wrote this book to remind you that life is meant to be *lived* with playfulness, presence and a big, bold heart.

I'm not here to preach or give you a rigid plan. I'm here to share my journey, the messy, joyful and sometimes chaotic path to learning how to show up fully, whether you're an introvert who wants to step out more or an extrovert who needs to slow down and be mindful.

This book is a celebration of all the ways we can take up space, connect deeply, move freely and create rituals that ground us amid the noise.

It's written in a simple, friendly style—no jargon, no heavy theory—just real stories and practical ideas you can start using today to make your life more playful, creative and full of wonder.

So get ready. You're about to dive into a joyful, messy, vibrant journey—one that invites you to live louder, love bigger and play harder.

*Let's get started!*

# Life's Not Waiting—Why Should You?

Let's get one thing straight—I'm not here to sell you a recovery arc.

I wasn't living under a rock. I wasn't afraid of people. I wasn't shy. I've always been out there—creating, expressing, exploring and doing. But what I've realised is that even movement can be unconscious. Even action can be noisy but hollow.

We can say "yes" to everything and still feel disconnected.

We can be loud on the outside and still foggy inside.

We can be in motion, but not living.

This book is an invitation to both the doers and the dreamers.

- If you tend to stay in your head, this is a nudge to *get in the game*.
- If you're already in the game, this is a call to *play with intention*.

I'm not offering rules or life hacks.

What I'm offering is a reminder: your aliveness is sacred, and it deserves your presence.

## This Book Is For You If

- You're an introvert who's mastered comfort, but not connection.
- You're an extrovert who's always busy, but sometimes wonders, "What for?"

- You've done the work—read the quotes, journalled the pain, vision-boarded the dream—but something still feels missing.
- You know that living isn't the same as being *fully engaged.*

And most importantly: You're ready to meet life not with control, or caution, or calculation, but with a sense of playfulness.

## What You'll Find Inside

Stories. Reflections. Messy truths. Mindful action. And a little magic.

Each chapter will take you into a theme—like overthinking, people, passion, solitude, or the body—and guide you to:

- Reflect
- Move
- Play with your edges

Because life isn't just to be survived or even mastered. *It's to be danced with.*

# Contents

| | |
|---|---|
| **Dedication** | iii |
| **About the Author** | iv |
| **Author's Note** | vi |
| **Let's Play!** | vii |
| **Life's Not Waiting—Why Should You?** | viii |
| **The Stuckness of Safety (Even in Motion)** | 1 |
| **Absorbing Isn't Living** | 7 |
| **Stop Fixing Yourself — Start Playing** | 12 |
| **The Power of Stories in Healing** | 17 |
| **Take Up Space, Even If It Feels Weird** | 21 |
| **The Art of Saying Yes Without Losing Yourself** | 25 |
| **Embrace the Weird—Your Unique Self Is Your Superpower** | 29 |
| **The Playful Mindset—How to Turn Life Into a Game** | 33 |
| **Energy-Rich Relationships—Connecting Without Exhaustion** | 37 |
| **Create Your Own Rituals—Anchors in the Playful Storm** | 41 |
| **Celebrate Small Wins—The Fuel for Playful Living** | 44 |
| **Playful Productivity—Getting Things Done Without Burning Out** | 47 |
| **"No" Is a Tiny Word with Superpowers** | 52 |
| **Playful Mindfulness—Being Present Without Pressure** | 56 |
| **Bringing It All Together—Your Playful Life Blueprint** | 59 |
| **The "What If This Were a Game?" Trick** | 69 |

| | |
|---|---|
| **Invite Your Inner Mischief** | **70** |
| **Play with Senses** | **71** |
| **Let Go of the Outcome** | **72** |
| **Build a Character for a Day** | **73** |
| **Add a Surprise to Routine** | **74** |
| **Invite Someone to Play** | **75** |
| **Design a 10-Minute Play Break** | **76** |
| **Your Play Philosophy** | **77** |
| **The Playful Living Toolkit** | **78** |
| **Note of Gratitude** | **80** |

**CHAPTER 1**

# The Stuckness of Safety (Even in Motion)

## My Story

When I quit my corporate job and stepped into the unknown, I quickly realised that being my own boss wasn't as simple as it sounded. I'd sit on the couch, waiting for inspiration to strike, hoping that watching a show, reading, or listening to a podcast would magically spark my next big idea.

But creativity didn't come knocking at my door—it showed up when I started doing something. One day, I made myself lunch, then decided to try out a dessert recipe I'd been curious about. That simple act led to planning a picnic, and at that picnic, my friends and I ended up jamming and writing a song together. The energy of active engagement unlocked a flow that sitting still never could.

What changed was—when I caught myself overthinking, retreating mentally or waiting for motivation, I consciously shifted gears and instead chose to play and engage by saying say *yes* to small, seemingly unrelated moments and to just show up. It wasn't about forcing productivity or perfection—it was about letting the pieces move, even if slowly, and trusting the process. This shift opened doors to joy, creativity and connection that no amount of passive waiting ever would.

Emotionally, embracing this playful, engaging approach felt like finding a missing puzzle piece. Each small, mundane moment wasn't wasted time but part of a larger picture coming into focus.

Like a puzzle, when you look at each piece alone, it may seem insignificant, but together they form something meaningful. And even if one piece is missing, the puzzle isn't complete—every piece holds value. That realisation helped me welcome every moment, every choice, as part of my vibrant, engaged life.

## So, What Is Stuckness?

Let's be honest—most of us are doing a lot. Plans. Projects. People. Posts. Some of us are out every weekend, and others are deep in their inner world. Some are multitasking queens, others are deep thinkers with multiple tabs open in their minds. But busy isn't the same as alive, and rest isn't always the same as renewal.

This isn't about doing more or less. It's about doing what matters—and noticing when safety or comfort becomes a disguise for not moving forward.

*"Sometimes the prison is not made of bars, but of comfort zones."*

## Not All Stillness Is Peaceful

You know that feeling when you're home, phone in hand, swiping, snacking, chilling—but there's a faint buzz of disconnection underneath? That's not peace. That's "pause" with no "play". That's what I call the stuckness of safety.

It looks different for everyone:

Saying no to every plan with a "Maybe next week".

Being booked and busy, but feeling hollow inside.

Comfort food, comfort content and conversations that don't really go anywhere.

We think we're being wise, calm and protective of our space, but sometimes, we're just checked out.

## How I Caught Myself

I'm someone who loves doing things. I thrive on expression. I'm not shy or withdrawn. But there were days I'd be doing everything except what lights me up. I'd meet ten people, but not have one real conversation. I'd create something, but I'd feel numb after posting it. I was "on", but not *in*. It wasn't depression. It wasn't anxiety. It was just being disconnected, drifting away from presence. And that, too, is stuckness.

## Engagement Isn't Just About Showing Up—It's About How You Show Up

It's easy to confuse motion with meaning. But here's the truth: You can be very active and still be unavailable to life. And you can be silent, yet deeply alive inside.

So I stopped asking, 'Am I doing enough?' and started asking, 'Am I engaged right now?' That single shift changed everything.

## The Deeper Why

The brain is wired to seek safety over change—even if that "safety" is actually a form of stuckness. Psychologically, this is known as homeostasis—our mind-body system prefers familiar discomfort over unfamiliar freedom. We may appear busy or in motion, but unless our internal compass feels safe enough to explore, true movement—emotional, creative, or spiritual—stalls. Noticing this is the first act of courage.

## Mini Pause: How Are You Showing Up?

Take a moment and check in. Right now, are you in:

- Auto-pilot?
- Over-functioning?

- Avoidance-in-comfort-mode?
- Or actually here, with breath, presence and curiosity?

No shame. Just notice.

## So, What Does Engagement Look Like?

It looks like:

- Responding instead of reacting.
- Being intentional with your yeses and your silences.
- Making space for joy and weirdness—not just hustle or healing.
- Letting life feel like a co-creation, not a task list.

It doesn't mean chasing every opportunity or fixing yourself. It means plugging in again—to the moment, to yourself, to the people in front of you.

## Try This to Snap Out of Stuckness

Pick one this week:

- Do something with full presence. Doesn't matter what—watering a plant, a phone call, dancing in your room. But do it with every cell in your body awake.
- Say yes to something unplanned. Not because you "should", but because it lights a spark.
- Catch yourself mid-scroll or mid-task—and ask, "Do I want to be here?" If yes, enjoy. If no, shift.

## Reflect

- Where in your life are you active but unengaged?
- What's your version of "safe but stuck"?
- What small, playful action could crack that shell open?

# A Simple Framework

*You don't need a life overhaul.*
*You don't need to become a new person.*

You just need to meet your life again—not with the heaviness of fixing or improving, but with the lightness of rediscovery.

Meet it with:

## Approaching with Curiosity and Intention

Approach your everyday routines with fresh eyes. Let go of the autopilot. Ask small questions: *What do I feel drawn to today? What am I noticing? What's changing around me?*

Curiosity turns even the mundane into mystery. It invites you to observe instead of judge, explore instead of conclude.

Intention isn't about control or perfection. It's about choosing presence. It's the quiet clarity that says, 'This is what matters to me right now.'

Start small: a five-minute mindful moment, a walk without your phone, a deliberate "yes" or a courageous "no." Intention anchors you amidst the chaos.

## Energy – *Not Hustle, But Vitality*

This isn't about doing more. It's about noticing what gives you life, and giving it space. Energy flows when you are in alignment, not when you're constantly pushing.

Choose nourishing inputs: movement, good company, nature, laughter and rest. Create little bursts of momentum by honouring your rhythms, not overriding them.

## Play – *The Shortcut to Joy*

You were wired for play—not just as a child, but as a human. Play is not a luxury. It's your access to freedom, spontaneity and connection.

It can look like silliness, creativity, exploration, or simply doing something *just because it delights you.* Play dissolves resistance and makes room for flow.

## You don't need a new life—just a new lens.

Meet your life like a traveller who has returned home—surprised by its beauty, curious about its corners and grateful for what was there all along.

You in?

# CHAPTER 2

# Absorbing Isn't Living

## From Observing to Contributing

When I first moved to Bangalore, I was instantly captivated by the city's buzzing energy. I dove headfirst into events, gatherings and meetups—not just to soak up inspiration, but to find mentors who could broaden my world. I met artists displaying their work in galleries, hosts running unique homestays and people leading cultural and travel events. Each encounter was a treasure trove of learning, and I eagerly absorbed everything, feeling part of a vibrant, inspiring community.

But over time, I realised something important: being a cheerful observer wasn't enough. As my own experiences deepened and my personality blossomed, I wanted to share my unique voice, not just learn from others. So I started writing more, painting more and building community in ways that felt authentic to me. I began hosting potlucks and opening my home as a gallery space, creating a place where people could engage directly with my work and vision.

A huge part of my engagement journey was with the *Happy Wall Project*, where I reached out to schools, underprivileged communities and corporate CSR teams to collaborate on creating uplifting wall art. It wasn't always easy—there were challenges in coordinating between different groups and making sure everyone's voice was heard—but step by step, we built something meaningful together.

From that project, a community slowly took shape. People began connecting, sharing their stories and supporting one another. Over time, this network grew into a group that continues to encourage me and each other to stay engaged, creative and connected. Building this community showed me that engagement is an ongoing effort, one that grows stronger when nurtured with patience and genuine connection.

## When Consuming Becomes a Trap

We live in a world of mass information consumption.

Reels. Podcasts. Tweets. Opinions. Advice.

Self-help. Self-soothing. Self-analysis.

We're full of other people's voices, ideas and aesthetics.

But here's the quiet truth: *you can absorb the entire internet and still feel hollow* because absorption isn't engagement. And consumption isn't connection.

We think: "Let me just scroll a bit, watch something calm, read something inspiring, then I'll feel better." But often, we just feel more drained. Why? Because we're inputting more than we're expressing, and taking in more than we're exchanging.

Sitting still—but not resting. It's like listening to a hundred songs but never singing one yourself.

The shift, from absorbing energy to actively giving it, changed everything. When I put my energy out into the world, the returns were profound: deeper connections, a stronger sense of purpose and a joyful flow of creative exchange. It taught me that true growth and fulfilment come when you bring your own light to the table, creating a dance of give and take that energises everyone involved.

## The Energy Exchange Principle

Here's a little truth I live by now: *energy moves when you move it.*

You don't get more life-force by taking it in, you get it by putting something out—an idea, a laugh, a dance or a hello.

Whether you're an introvert or an extrovert, life expands when you exchange energy, not just sit with it. Even making a cup of tea for someone is more energising than binge-watching someone else's perfect routine.

## You're Not a Sponge. You're a Spark.

You were not meant to soak up the world in silence. You were meant to interact with it.

Respond to it.

Shape it.

Absorbing other people's brilliance can spark something, yes. But, when you respond—create, speak, sing, move—that's when the magic happens.

So if you've been watching life like a movie, maybe it's time to get up and join the scene.

## The Problem with "Just One More"

One more video.

One more article.

One more quote that might change your life.

You think you're "gathering energy", but energy doesn't come from hoarding inspiration—it comes from movement and from creating, expressing, responding and interacting. It's not about what you consume—*it's about what you contribute.*

## The Deeper Why

Passive consumption—whether it's scrolling, watching or endlessly reading—can create an illusion of living without the emotional engagement that real experience demands.

Psychologically, this is a form of *dissociation*, where the mind observes but doesn't participate. To shift from absorbing to living, we need embodiment—being fully present in our senses, choices and actions. That's where life truly begins to feel real.

## Mini Pause: Check Your Input to Output Ratio

Ask yourself:

- How much am I taking in today?
- How much am I putting out—even if it's something small and silly?
- Am I consuming more than I'm connecting?
- Learning but not applying?
- Admiring others but withholding my own brilliance?

Just observe. Awareness alone is gold.

## Try This and Flip the Script

For the next 3 days:

- For every hour of input, do 10 minutes of output.
- Read something? Write a thought about it.
- Watched something? Talk to someone about how it moved you.
- Listened to music? Move to it. Sing with it. Do something.

- Create something before you consume—a note, a sketch, a voice memo, a reel, a dance, or a meal.
- Connect instead of scrolling—message someone, share a memory, ask a real question.

Human energy > algorithmic comfort.

## Reflect

- Where am I using input as a distraction instead of inspiration?
- What voice within me is longing to be heard?
- What do I need to stop absorbing so I can start living?

## Reminder

You don't need more content—you need contact.

With yourself. With others. With the world around you.

You're not a sponge, you're a flame. And flames don't absorb, they glow.

Glowing isn't about perfection! It's not about becoming a better version of yourself through endless tweaking, fixing and optimising.

It's about being fully present—messy, alive and lit from within.

The truth is: you don't need fixing.

You need to *feel* again.

And the easiest way back to feeling?

Play.

# CHAPTER 3

# Stop Fixing Yourself — Start Playing

## From Achievement to Stuckness

After writing my first book, *Think Build Create*, I thought I had crossed the biggest hurdle. Surely, now I could call myself an author, and the rest—recognition, success, fulfilment—would follow naturally.

Instead, I found myself staring at metrics, planning marketing strategies, reaching out to collaborators and wondering what came next. At 35, I wasn't where I imagined I'd be. The book was out in the world, but I was caught in the quiet in-between—no longer chasing a dream, not yet building a new one.

That limbo led me somewhere unexpected: my childhood.

## Reclaiming Play

I remembered how much joy I used to feel listening to cassette-storybooks as a child. I still have a treasured collection of beautifully illustrated children's books. Then the idea struck: *what if I wrote children's books?*

That whimsical spark pulled me out of the spiral. It didn't come from deep introspection or strategy—it came from curiosity. I stopped trying to figure it all out and started following what felt fun.

What followed was *Magic Ink*—a series of children's stories I had already written but never shared. Turning them into audiobooks with the help of a team brought the joy of collaboration and fresh creative momentum. I wasn't waiting anymore, I was creating again—because I was playing again.

## You Are Not a Problem to Be Solved

We've been taught to pause our lives until we've fixed ourselves.

*Fix your mindset.*
*Heal your past.*
*Raise your vibration.*
*Glow up. Level up. Show up.*

It's an endless upgrade cycle, and it leaves us feeling like a never-finished project.

But here's the truth:
You don't need to be "better" to begin.
You just need to *begin.* Start with what brings you joy.

You are allowed to be a little messy and still create meaning.
You're allowed to feel unfinished and still deeply alive.

## When Inner Work Becomes a Delay Tactic

Self-awareness is valuable. Growth is beautiful. But when "working on ourselves" becomes an excuse to delay action, connection or creation—it becomes a trap.

We say:

"I need to feel more confident first."
"Maybe I should read one more book."
"Maybe I need to process this fully before I start…"

I've done my share of internal reflection—what I call "inner engineering". This process has helped me observe my thoughts, manage my energy and feel grounded no matter what's happening externally. It's powerful and necessary.

But it's not the destination, it's the foundation.

Inner clarity is what *frees* you to engage more joyfully with the world, not avoid it. When you're grounded from within, you're more willing to take risks, show up, share and collaborate.

That's where play comes in—it's the bridge between your inner world and the outer one.

And slowly, life becomes less of a spectator sport and more of a creative workshop.

Here's a truth I've learned: you don't always need more *inner work*. You often need more *outer play*.

## Manifestation: Align, Then Act

Let's talk about manifestation—not as a buzzword, but as a tool.

To me, it's not about wishing and waiting. It's about *clarity*. Manifestation helps you strip away the noise and say: *this is what I really want*. It aligns your energy, thoughts, and intentions in one direction.

But that's just the starting point.

After clarity comes movement. You don't manifest something by thinking alone—you make it real by acting. You get up, try, stumble and show up again.

Vision without action is just fantasy.

Vision with action?

That's manifestation.

## The Deeper Why

Constant self-improvement can quietly reinforce the belief that you're broken. Psychologists call this the "self-discrepancy theory", where the gap between who you are and who you think you *should* be becomes a source of chronic anxiety.

But play interrupts this pattern. It lets you engage with life from curiosity, not criticism. And that shift—from fixing to exploring—is where real healing begins.

## Pause & Ask

*What are you postponing in the name of self-improvement?*

- What playful thing have you delayed because you're "not ready"?
- In what aspects are you waiting to be more healed, more polished, more complete before showing up?

Remember: you are not incomplete. You are *in motion*.

## Try This: Act Before You're Ready

- Do something joyful that makes no logical sense—sing badly, paint wildly, wear that outfit you are "saving for later".
- Give yourself one full day without fixing or analysing yourself.
- Let your body, voice and hands express what your mind is still processing.

Let play be your mirror—not your to-do list.

## Reflect

- What parts of you come alive when you stop trying to "improve"?
- Where has "self-work" delayed self-expression?
- What would it feel like to be unapologetically in motion?

We often underestimate the healing power of joy.

- Play brings presence.
- Presence brings healing.
- Healing builds confidence.
- Confidence creates clarity.

You don't always need a five-step plan.

Sometimes you just need to laugh, dance, try something weird and surprise yourself.

There's wisdom in whimsy, if you let it move you.

## A Soft Reminder

You are not an algorithm waiting to be optimised.
You are not a flaw to be corrected.
You are not a never-ending project.

You are a spark, a rhythm, a story in motion.

So stop fixing and start playing.

That's where the real transformation begins.

# CHAPTER 4
# The Power of Stories in Healing

There are days when I just don't know what to do with myself—when everything feels foggy, uninspired and heavy. On those days, I've learned that the best thing I can do is simply get out of the house. No big plans, no pressure to be productive—just move. A short walk, a coffee run, jumping jacks or skipping with an invisible rope—anything. Movement shifts something. It tells my body that I am safe, that I'm still here, that I can breathe again.

I started exploring movement not as exercise, but as a tool to move my mood. Ecstatic dance, for example, became a beautiful discovery—no choreography, no expectations—just raw, unfiltered expression through the body. The first time I tried it, I felt nervous and awkward. But as the music played and the people around me let go, I followed. I jumped, I swayed, I spun and something opened. Movement helped me return to myself; it released the mental noise. And in that physical release, I found clarity, softness and often—surprisingly—creative spark.

## The Body's Secret Language

You know that feeling when you're stuck?

When your mind is racing, dragging, or flatlining?

When all the thinking in the world feels like shouting into an empty room?

Here's something we often forget:
*Your body is your first gateway back to life.*

Before clarity, before words, before solutions—your body already knows what to do. It holds a deep intelligence.

Your body remembers what your mind forgets.

Stress curls your shoulders.
Sadness slows your breath.
Joy makes your heart beat faster.

When you move your body—even a little—you begin to shift your internal weather.
A walk outside can clear mental fog.
Stretching can release tension you didn't know you were holding.
Dancing like no one's watching can crack open a smile you thought was lost.

Movement reminds your system that you're alive. It sends the message: I'm here. I'm listening. I'm okay.

## Moving Is How You Show Up for Yourself

Sitting still with a swirling mind can feel like being trapped in a box.

Movement is how you step outside that box—into presence, into possibility.

When you move, you create space—not just in your body, but in your inner world.

Movement doesn't need to be intense or complicated; it just needs to be honest.

You don't have to get it "right", you just have to get going.

Movement is more than physical exercise—it's a doorway to emotional release, nervous system regulation and self-connection. By reconnecting with your body, you begin to loosen stories, soften resistance and shift your state from within. Healing, it turns out, doesn't have to be loud or logical—it can be rhythmic, simple and deeply embodied. You don't have to figure it out—you can move through it.

*"The simplest step forward is often a step outside."*

## The Deeper Why

The body and mind are deeply linked—so much so that movement can change your emotional state faster than thought alone. Psychologists refer to this as *embodied cognition*: your body doesn't just respond to your emotions, it helps create them. Even small, playful movements send signals of aliveness to the brain, shifting mood, energy and outlook. In motion, we often meet ourselves again.

This is why somatic practices—like mindful movement, breathwork and body-based therapy—are so powerful. They remind us that healing isn't always about talking or thinking; sometimes, it's about *feeling* through the body what the mind can't explain.

## Pause: What's Your Movement?

- When was the last time you moved just to feel good—not to burn calories or fix something?
- What kind of movement does your body crave today? Something slow and grounding or wild and freeing?
- What's one small, kind movement you can offer your body right now?

## Try Movement as Medicine

### For the next 3 days:

- Move for 5 minutes before any big decision or focused work. Dance, stretch, walk, jump—whatever feels natural. Then pause and notice how your mind responds.
- Identify one "stuck" moment each day—a time when your mood dips or your energy feels blocked. Stop, breathe and do a quick body shift: shake out your arms, roll your shoulders, sway side to side.
- Reclaim play and move like a child, an animal, a wave—just for the joy of it. No goal. No judgment. Just presence.

### Reflect

- What happens to my thoughts and emotions when I move before thinking?
- When do I stop myself from moving because of old "shoulds" or stories?
- What becomes possible when I let my body lead the way?

### A Quiet Reminder

Your body is more than a machine—it's a compass. A memory keeper. A healing partner. When the mind gets lost or overwhelmed, the body can bring you back.

So when in doubt, don't just sit there.

Move. Stretch. Shake. Dance. Breathe.

Let your body lead you home.

# CHAPTER 5

# Take Up Space, Even If It Feels Weird

## Being Multi-Passionate Isn't Scattered

I spent a lot of my life trying to shrink. Not just in physical space, but in presence. I thought if I toned myself down, if I became easier to digest, I'd be more accepted, more successful and more loved. But here's the truth I've come to realise: you don't benefit from becoming smaller—it flourishes when you expand.

As someone who has always juggled multiple interests—singing, writing, teaching, designing—I used to feel like I was "too much". I even had people around me imply it, but I've learned that being multi-passionate isn't a flaw—it's actually a strength. It took me years of unlearning to see it that way.

Writing my book, *Meera and the Magic Kolam,* was one of the first times I allowed myself to fully step into my creative potential. I didn't wait for validation. I didn't try to make it small—I just created it with joy. Later, when I started the Multipotentialite Meetups, I saw I wasn't alone. So many others were quietly trying to break themselves out of boxes they'd outgrown.

## The Deeper Why

Many of us have internalised the idea that visibility is dangerous or selfish. Psychologically, this traces back to *fawn responses*—a survival mechanism where we minimise ourselves to avoid conflict or rejection. We shrink because we think it will make life easier. Because we've internalised the idea that humility means invisibility. Because someone once told us to stop showing off. Because the world often applauds people who are quiet, accommodating and low-maintenance. Taking up space can feel uncomfortable at first because it challenges old safety patterns, but with each bold step, your nervous system begins to learn: *it's safe to be seen.*

But playing small doesn't protect you; it erodes you.

I've seen it time and again—not just in myself, but in friends, colleagues and even students. We hold back brilliant ideas and apologise before we speak. We dull our sparkle in rooms where it could light things up. The irony is, the very thing we're trying to hide is often the thing the world most needs from us.

## Choosing Expansion

Expansion feels awkward at first. Walking into a room like you belong there, standing up straight, owning your voice—it all feels foreign if you've spent years doing the opposite.

But taking up space is a muscle, and like any muscle, it strengthens with use.

**Start with this:** Allow yourself to be seen fully in one area of your life. Maybe it's wearing the outfit you secretly love, saying no without apologising or finally launching that side project you've talked yourself out of.

Here's a simple truth I've learned: not everyone will clap when you expand. Some people will be uncomfortable. Some will criticise.

But that's not your burden to carry. Your only responsibility is to show up as your full self.

## Try to Expand in Action

Here are a few exercises that helped me step into my own space more confidently:

- **Mirror Power Pose**: Every morning, stand in front of the mirror, shoulders back, chin up. Hold a power pose for two minutes and say one thing you love about yourself. It's scientifically-backed—it actually boosts confidence.
- **Speak Without Softening**: Notice how often you say things like "I just feel..." or "I could be wrong but...". Try stating your thoughts directly; you'll be surprised at how it changes your energy.
- **Claim Your Wins**: Keep a "Brag Book"—a notebook or some notes on your phone where you write down compliments, wins and moments where you felt proud. Revisit it on days you're shrinking.
- **Follow Expansive People**: Fill your feed and bookshelf with people who live boldly—artists, writers, thinkers who inspire you to be more, not less. One quote I love is from author Elizabeth Gilbert: *"Don't abandon your creativity the moment things stop being easy or rewarding. Because that's the moment when the interesting begins."*

## Ask yourself:

- In what situations do I feel like I shrink myself or hold back?
- Around whom do I notice I make myself smaller?
- What would it feel like to take up a little more space, in body and in voice?

## Grounding Thoughts

Taking up space isn't about arrogance—it's about alignment. It's about standing tall in your truth, even when it wobbles. It's about being visible, not for ego, but for freedom.

So go ahead—be bold, be bright, be fully, unapologetically you. Even if it feels weird—*especially then*.

# CHAPTER 6

# The Art of Saying Yes Without Losing Yourself

## Improv: Learning to Say Yes to the Unknown

The first time I stepped into an improv class, I didn't know what I was signing up for. I had signed up for a theatre class, not realising improv would be a big part of it. But I was there.

There's one golden rule in improv: *say yes*. Yes, to whatever comes your way. Yes, to the unpredictable. Yes, to the scene your partner starts. Yes, to the weird character you're suddenly supposed to become. In improv, you don't have time to second-guess or plan. You simply receive and respond.

This principle seeped into my life. It started with small things: attending random events, saying "yes" to conversations with strangers and trying new experiences outside my comfort zone. What surprised me was how this seemingly silly theatre technique helped me feel more open and courageous in real life. My confidence grew—not because I had everything figured out, but because I was practising trust. Trust in myself. Trust in the moment.

## Travel: Taking Yes on the Road

My big "yes" moment came when I travelled solo to Rajasthan. I didn't have a tight itinerary. I just said yes to whatever showed up: joining a local dance group for a night of celebration, trying unfamiliar food, getting lost in the streets of Jaisalmer and being invited to a puppet-making workshop.

I found myself talking to strangers in cafes, sharing stories with fellow travellers and even facilitating small workshops in communities I stumbled upon. There was something magical about that phase of my life—like I had finally understood how to live fully. Saying "yes" cracked me open in the best way.

But it wasn't always perfect. Saying yes too often started to drain me. I became so addicted to newness that I began ignoring signs of fatigue. I didn't want to miss out. I feared that if I said no, I'd lose momentum, or worse, become boring. That's when I had to pause and ask myself: Is this aligned with joy or just fear of missing out?

## Energy Check: When Yes Becomes Too Much

The thing about always saying yes is—it's unsustainable. At first, it feels exciting. You're expanding. But left unchecked, it turns into overwhelm. I began losing touch with my own rhythm. I was so eager to be open to life that I forgot to ask: do I actually want this?

That's when I started doing regular energy check-ins. Before saying yes, I'd pause and ask:

*Is this a yes from excitement or pressure?*

*Is this a yes that adds joy or drains me later?*

Through these questions, I began to refine my yes. I realised that saying yes doesn't mean saying yes to everything. It means saying yes wholeheartedly—to the things that matter, that light you up and that move you toward your most alive self.

## Saying Yes Selectively

Now, I use what I call a "joy filter." If something excites me—even if it scares me—I lean in. But if something feels heavy, forced, or like I'm doing it to please others, I give myself permission to step back.

This shift didn't just protect my energy—it sharpened my intuition. I became more *intentional*. I noticed which projects gave me energy and which ones drained me. I was able to notice who I truly enjoyed spending time with. My "yes" started to feel powerful, not performative.

One way to develop this filter is by tracking your "full yes" moments. *What were you doing? Who were you with? How did it feel?* Patterns will emerge. The more you honour those patterns, the more your life begins to reflect your values.

And here's something fascinating: research shows that saying yes to new experiences can activate brain regions linked to reward and motivation. So, the magic you feel when you try something new? It's real. It's your brain lighting up with possibility.

## The Deeper Why

Saying yes can feel like connection—but when it overrides your truth, it becomes self-abandonment. Psychologically, this often stems from *people-pleasing*, a learned strategy to gain approval and avoid rejection. The real art is in saying yes from wholeness, not fear. Each authentic yes reinforces your sense of self, rather than dissolving it.

## Mini Pause

Before saying yes, ask yourself:

- Am I excited for this or just scared to say no?
- Is this choice aligned with my values?
- Will this bring me energy or leave me depleted?

## Try to Track Your Full Yes Moments

- For one week, write down moments that felt like a clear, energising yes.
- Note where you were, who was involved, and how you felt afterwards.
- At the end of the week, look for patterns. What do your yeses have in common?

## Reflect

- Do you tend to say yes out of fear or out of joy?
- What does your inner yes feel like? Where do you feel it in your body?
- Is there something you've been hesitating to say yes to? What's stopping you?

## Reminder

Saying yes isn't about being available to everyone and everything. It's about being available to your growth, joy and expansion.

Let your yes come from clarity, not compulsion.

**Grounding Thought:** The art of saying "yes" is not about doing more—it's about choosing more consciously. When your yes comes from a place of deep truth, it opens the right doors and keeps you connected to who you really are.

## CHAPTER 7

# Embrace the Weird—Your Unique Self Is Your Superpower

**My Journey with Weirdness**

For the longest time, I felt like I was a bit "too much" for the world around me. Too expressive, too emotional and too dreamy. I often tried to tone it down—to fit in, blend in, stay safe. I'd see people respond with puzzled looks or awkward silences when I shared my quirky ideas or dramatic impressions. I felt like I had to hide the real me to be liked.

In school, I was known as the girl who sang at lunch break or scribbled stories in the back of her notebook. While some found it entertaining, others found it strange. I remember once being told, 'You're so weird,' and not knowing whether it was meant as an insult or a compliment. Back then, I took it as the former. I thought being different was dangerous.

But over time, especially as I entered creative spaces—workshops, writing groups, music circles—I found people who didn't just accept my weirdness, they celebrated it. In fact, they had their own brand of weird, too! And that's when it clicked: *this so-called weirdness wasn't something to fix—it was my strength.* The more I leaned into it, the more confident and authentic I became.

## Why Weirdness is a Strength

We live in a world that often praises sameness, but the truth is, *all great creativity and innovation has come from people who were brave enough to be different.*

Whether it's Steve Jobs obsessing over typography when building Apple, or Lady Gaga owning her bold fashion and sound, the ones who stood out stood tall. They didn't let the world water them down; they instead leaned into their unique essence, and the world eventually caught up.

Think of Steve Jobs—a college dropout, barefoot in boardrooms, obsessed with design and simplicity. He didn't follow trends; he set them. Or Lady Gaga, who wore meat dresses and sang anthems for the misfits. Her boldness wasn't a gimmick — it was a declaration: *This is me, exactly as I am.*

Or Frida Kahlo, who painted her pain, her politics and her unapologetic identity onto every canvas. Prince, who blurred the lines of gender, genre and fashion. David Bowie, who shapeshifted his way through art and music while never losing the core of his strange brilliance.

They didn't dim their difference—they amplified it.

They weren't always understood—but they were always *themselves.*

When you embrace your unique qualities, you unlock authenticity. And authenticity is magnetic. It allows people to connect with the real you. Your weirdness—quirks, preferences, passions and ways of thinking—are the colours that make your canvas vivid.

And let's be real: it's exhausting to constantly shrink yourself. Pretending to be something you're not takes energy. On the other hand, *being yourself is liberating.* You free up energy to create, connect and grow.

We often spend years trying to "belong" by blending in, but the truth is, the people who change the world, or even just light up a room, don't do it by conforming. They do it by owning what makes them different. Their quirks, their vision and their style—the very things that might have made them outcasts once—became their power.

Your uniqueness might not look like Steve Jobs, Lady Gaga, or Frida Kahlo, but it has just as much power. The question is: Are you willing to stop editing yourself and start expressing yourself?

## How to Embrace Your Weird in Everyday Life

Here's the thing—embracing your uniqueness doesn't mean shouting from rooftops. Sometimes it's as simple as wearing that bold scarf you love, speaking your mind in a meeting, or dancing like nobody's watching (because really, no one is).

You start with small, safe spaces—maybe with a trusted friend or a supportive community. You share that poem, sing that song, pitch that wild idea. With every act of self-expression, you build a stronger relationship with yourself.

## The Deeper Why

The drive to "fit in" is hardwired—our brains are wired for belonging. But what often gets called "weird" is just authenticity that hasn't been normalised. Psychologists call this *differentiation*: the ability to stay connected to others while staying true to yourself. Embracing your uniqueness isn't rebellion—it's maturity.

## Here are a few prompts and tools to get you started:

### Pause and Reflect:

- What parts of you have you dimmed or hidden to fit in?
- What would happen if you gave them a little space to breathe?

### Try This Activity

Create a "Weird and Wonderful" list. Write down five things that make you different—the things you love, your unusual talents or habits you used to feel shy about. Now, write how each one has helped you connect, create or thrive.

### Reflect

Think of a time you showed up as your full self and felt good about it. What did you do? Who were you with? What helped you feel safe? That's a clue to the environments you thrive in.

### Grounding Thought

If I could go back and tell my younger self one thing, it would be this: You're not too much, you're exactly enough. What makes you different is what makes you powerful. It's time to stop dimming your light and start dancing in it.

You don't need to appeal to everyone. The right people will appreciate you for who you are—not a watered-down version of yourself. Your authenticity acts like a lighthouse—it naturally attracts your kind of people.

So let the world adjust to you, not the other way around. Because the truth is—*your uniqueness is your superpower.*

# CHAPTER 8

# The Playful Mindset—How to Turn Life Into a Game

There was a time when I found myself stuck. I had left my corporate job, but the joy I thought I'd find in freedom didn't come rushing in. Instead, I fell into a dull routine. Life felt heavier than before. Every morning, I woke up with a sense of obligation rather than excitement, moving through tasks like ticking boxes. Something vital had gone missing—the spark, the spontaneity, the *play*.

Eventually, I started to see that what I missed wasn't structure or pressure. It was *aliveness*. Not the kind that comes from big achievements, but the kind that arises when we're simply having fun. Slowly, without realising it, I began to infuse small moments with play—dancing while brushing my teeth, narrating my chores in a dramatic voice, or inventing silly songs while cooking. At first, it felt a bit ridiculous. But over time, it transformed my entire day.

*Play isn't something we grow out of—it's something we forget and must return to.*

Somewhere along the way, many of us started equating adulthood with seriousness. We began believing that play is only for children, or that it's an indulgence rather than a necessity.

But what if play is the missing ingredient that makes everyday life not just bearable, but *joyful*?

## Play in the Everyday

We tend to think of play as something that happens on a holiday or during a hobby, but it can be embedded right into our routines. You can find micro-moments to inject humour, curiosity, or wonder—even in the dullest situations. You can make up characters while cooking, race the clock while folding clothes, or even invent a backstory for the people in line at the store.

It's not about performing or producing—it's about shifting perspective. A task becomes less of a burden and more of a game.

Even the most ordinary parts of life—washing dishes, organising a drawer, waiting in traffic—can become spaces for creativity if we let them.

## What My Dog Taught Me

When my dog came into my life, I started to see how easily she turned the world into an adventure. A walk wasn't just a walk—it was a safari. A crumpled leaf became a treasure. Every new person was a potential friend. Her sheer delight in the present moment reminded me of what I'd forgotten: play isn't something separate from life; it *is* life, if we let it be.

She didn't care about outcomes. She didn't wait for the "right time" to feel joy. She followed instinct, curiosity and delight. Watching her was like getting a daily lesson in mindfulness and mischief.

## Why Play Matters

Play activates creativity, reduces stress and allows us to problem-solve without pressure. It helps us tap into flow—the state of ease and energy where ideas and solutions come naturally. More importantly, it connects us back to our essence—that part of us that is light, curious and alive.

But here's something to acknowledge: not everyone finds it easy to play. Some people feel awkward or guilty about it. After all, we've been trained to believe that being productive matters more than being playful. If that's you, start small. You don't have to turn into a cartoon character overnight. Begin with one moment—a funny voice, a doodle, a wiggle while stirring your tea—and see how it feels. The more you practice, the easier it becomes.

## The Deeper Why

A playful mindset helps the brain reframe challenges as opportunities rather than threats. This shift engages the *dopaminergic system*—the part of the brain that thrives on curiosity, novelty and reward. Psychologically, play reduces fear and increases problem-solving. When life becomes a game, it activates the creative, resilient parts of you that know how to adapt and flourish.

## Resisting Play

It's okay if part of you resists this idea. For many of us, play can feel silly, self-indulgent, or even unproductive, especially if we've been raised to believe that value comes from output, efficiency, or seriousness. But play isn't the opposite of work—it's what makes life more livable. It loosens the grip of perfectionism and restores energy. It reconnects us to joy without a scoreboard. If it feels unfamiliar, start small. Even one minute of lightness counts.

## Try to See Life as a Gameboard

Here are a few light-hearted ways to invite more play into your day. Think of them as rules in your own personal game of life.

- **Turn chores into missions:** Pretend you're on a timed quest while doing errands or cleaning.

- **Invent a character:** Go through part of your day pretending to be a pirate, a queen, or a film director.
- **Play with language:** Speak in rhymes, make up nonsense words, or narrate your thoughts like a sports commentator.
- **Change your environment:** Rearranging objects, lighting a candle, or playing a themed playlist can shift the mood and spark creativity.
- **Laugh at yourself:** Make a funny face in the mirror. Celebrate your mistakes like a game glitch.
- **Make a "just because" list:** Do something purely for the sake of joy, like colouring, singing off-key, or wearing something absurd.

These aren't about being silly for the sake of it. They're reminders that *you can shape the tone of your own day.*

## A Shift in Mindset

Play isn't just an action—it's a mindset, it's how you approach life. Instead of trudging through it like a to-do list, what if you danced through it like a puzzle or an adventure?

Play doesn't mean you aren't taking life seriously; it means you're choosing to experience it fully. Joyfully. Creatively. And often, that very joy leads to deeper productivity, stronger relationships and a sense of ease that no rigid schedule can provide.

## Your Turn

Today, try one playful thing. Just one.

Sing while cooking.

Talk in a ridiculous accent for five minutes.

Pretend you're the CEO of a wildly successful imaginary company.

Whatever it is—let yourself enjoy it. See what shifts. Because the world doesn't need perfect people, it needs people who are *alive*.

# CHAPTER 9

# Energy-Rich Relationships—Connecting Without Exhaustion

There was a time when I believed connection always had to come at the cost of energy. Like many of us, I had unknowingly trained myself to perform connection, to show up in a way that made others feel seen and heard, even if I was shrinking in the process. I was good at listening, holding space and adjusting myself to the needs of the people in the room. But often, I left these interactions feeling oddly drained, like I'd done a job rather than had a moment.

This chapter is about a new kind of connection—one that gives rather than takes, one where energy doesn't deplete, but expands, where showing up feels like a return to yourself instead of a departure.

## The People-Pleasing Trap

Many of us are conditioned to overextend ourselves in relationships, especially women, caregivers, or those from collectivist cultures. We're taught to read the room before we speak, to adjust our volume and tone, to smooth out our edges and make others feel comfortable. While this can create harmony, it can also create fatigue.

We forget to ask: *Is this connection nourishing me, too?*

When I began exploring the idea of energy-rich relationships, I noticed how some people left me feeling alive and buzzing, while others made me feel like I needed to lie down. It wasn't about good or bad people—it was about fit, timing, openness and honesty.

Think of yourself like a plant. You don't thrive just because you're surrounded by other plants; you thrive when you're placed in the right kind of light. Some relationships feel like the morning sun—they energise you, open you up, help you grow. Others cast a shadow, draining your strength even when you can't quite name why. This chapter is about learning to tell the difference.

## Why Connection Can Feel Draining

Sometimes, it's because:

- We're performing instead of being
- We're saying "yes" out of guilt
- We feel responsible for the emotional tone of the conversation
- We suppress our own truth to keep the peace
- We're overgiving without replenishment

But an energy-rich connection feels different:

- Shared laughter without effort
- Conversations that spark ideas
- Spaces where silence is allowed
- Relationships where boundaries are respected
- Being your weird, wonderful self without apology

## A Wider Lens

For some, even these nourishing connections may feel like a distant dream. If you're in a season of loneliness or in-betweenness, start small. Connection isn't always about people. It might be a song that moves you, a tree you greet daily, or a journal where you show up honestly. These small acts reconnect us to the world and to ourselves.

## Beyond Friendships

While most of my stories are rooted in friendships and creative spaces, this idea applies just as much to family, colleagues, or even online communities. Energy-rich connection isn't about the *type* of relationship—it's about *how* you show up in it.

## Deeper Why

At the heart of it, energy-rich relationships come from feeling safe—not just physically, but emotionally. When we're constantly managing, performing, or second-guessing ourselves around someone, our body quietly gets tired. Over time, it adds up. But when there's ease, honesty and space to be fully ourselves, something shifts. Psychologically, that's our nervous system telling us: 'You're okay here.' That's why the most energising relationships aren't always the loudest or the busiest—they're the ones where we can breathe.

## Try Energy Mapping

Over the next five days, track how you feel after interactions. Simply jot down:

- Whom did I speak to?
- How did I feel before?
- How did I feel after?
- Was the connection *energy-giving* or *energy-draining*?

Patterns will emerge. Use them. They are clues to where your spirit feels safe.

For the next five conversations you have—with a friend, colleague, family member, or stranger—pause afterwards and ask:

- How do I feel right now?
- More energised, more depleted, or neutral?
- What did that conversation ask of me—and what did it give me?

You might be surprised how clearly your body tells you which relationships are nourishing, and which are quietly costing you.

## Journal Prompt:

Make a list of five people or spaces that leave you feeling energised. Then make a list of five that drain you.

What do you notice?

What needs to shift?

## From Performance to Presence

Earlier, I shared how I used to perform connection. That old habit still returns sometimes, especially in work settings or high-stakes relationships. But now I pause and ask: *Is this me, or am I shape-shifting again?* It's not about cutting people off—it's about coming back to myself.

## Grounding Thoughts

Connection doesn't have to be exhausting. The right relationships won't require you to dim, contort, or overextend. They'll feel like light through an open window.

Let's stop confusing depletion with depth.

Let's stop calling burnout "belonging".

Let's find our people—the ones who fill us up, not drain us.

# CHAPTER 10
## Create Your Own Rituals—Anchors in the Playful Storm

I used to think rituals were just for serious, spiritual types—the kind who woke up at dawn, meditated for hours, or had a perfect morning routine. Me? I was all about spontaneity and flow, and sometimes that meant my days were a wild ride of chaos and creativity.

But then I noticed something: the days when I created little rituals—simple things I could count on—I felt grounded, even when life threw curveballs.

It started small, like lighting a candle before I sat down to write or play music, making a cup of herbal tea and sitting by the window to watch the world wake up, even just putting on a favourite song that instantly lifted my mood. These little anchors became my secret weapons against overwhelm and overthinking.

When the world feels like a playful storm, rituals help me catch my breath and come back to my centre.

I also realised rituals don't have to be complicated or rigid; they can be playful acts of self-love and presence. I know someone who draws a heart in the steam on their bathroom mirror every morning—a quiet ritual that reminds them to begin the day with love. Another friend lights a stick of sandalwood incense not for prayer, but as a way of saying, 'I'm home now.' It marks the shift from outside energy to inner calm.

These rituals signal that no matter how messy life gets, I'm showing up for me—creatively, mindfully, joyfully. And that simple commitment? It's a game-changer.

## Why Rituals Matter

Life throws curveballs, chaos comes knocking and sometimes, it feels like the world's spinning faster than you can catch. That's when rituals come to the rescue—little acts, repeated with intention, that ground you, centre you and invite you back to yourself.

Rituals aren't boring routines, they're purposeful pauses—moments to check in, recharge and reset. When life feels overwhelming, rituals are your anchor. They remind you who you are beneath all the noise.

## Rituals Are Playful, Too

Rituals don't have to be stiff or serious. They can be as simple as lighting a candle and dancing to your favourite song, or making a cup of tea and savouring every sip like it's a mini celebration.

The key?

Make them yours. Make them fun. Make them real.

## The Deeper Why

In a world that moves fast and often pulls us in many directions, rituals give the mind something to hold onto. Psychologically, they help regulate our emotions by offering rhythm, predictability and a sense of control—things our nervous system craves, especially during uncertainty. But the best rituals aren't always inherited or imposed—they're chosen. Crafted with intention, they become small, sacred pauses in the day that say: "You matter. You're safe. You're here."

## Mini Pause: What Rituals Speak to You?

Ask yourself:

- What small daily acts make me feel calm or joyful?
- Which moments do I want to turn into rituals?
- How can I bring a little playfulness into these rituals?

## Try to Create Your Own Ritual

- Pick one simple thing to do daily or weekly—a morning stretch, a gratitude note, a five-minute dance break.
- Make it playful by adding music, colour, or anything else that sparks joy.
- Keep it consistent enough to make you feel grounded, but flexible enough to stay fun.

## Reflect

- How do these rituals affect my mood and energy?
- What rituals help me feel connected to myself?
- How can I protect these moments from being rushed or skipped?

## Grounding Thoughts

Rituals aren't rules—they're your anchors, your calm in the storm and your way to hit the reset button and keep dancing through life.

# CHAPTER 11

# Celebrate Small Wins—The Fuel for Playful Living

There was a time I thought I could only celebrate when I got "there", to the big moment, the recognition and the prize. I would save my joy for when something truly worthy happened. Everything else was just "in between".

But the "there" kept moving.

No matter how many milestones I hit, the big bang I imagined never really came. So, I kept pushing, waiting and achieving, then waiting again, until I began to wonder—*what if the waiting never ends?*

That's when I decided to try something wildly new. I started celebrating the tiniest things—getting out of bed on time, responding to that one pending message and showing up for myself even when I didn't feel like it. And you know what? I began to feel full. *Joyful. Light.* As though I had secretly unlocked a reservoir of energy that was hiding in plain sight.

*I realised my story wasn't just personal—it was human. Most of us are waiting for a big reason to celebrate, without realising that joy doesn't need a stage.*

## Why Small Wins Matter

Small wins are the invisible fuel that powers us through the day. They're the breadcrumbs that lead us home when we feel lost.

When you notice and acknowledge them, it reinforces a sense of capability and momentum. You begin to trust yourself and start seeing progress in places you'd otherwise overlook.

It could be something as small as drinking enough water, saying no to something that drains you, or finally hitting 'send' on that uncomfortable email you've been putting off for days. These tiny triumphs are proof that you're showing up, even in life's quiet moments.

One day, I literally clapped for myself after hitting send on a long-overdue message that had been stressing me out. It felt silly, yet completely liberating. That tiny applause turned into a smile, and that smile turned into motivation to tackle the next task.

What's one "invisible win" you've had this week?

Celebrate it—even if it's just with a smile, a note to yourself, or a happy dance in your room.

## Progress Over Perfection

We often chase perfection, waiting for the most flawless version of ourselves to emerge before we feel proud. But perfection is a mirage. Progress, however, is real and worth celebrating.

By focusing on what's working, even in small doses, we create an emotional rhythm that encourages more of the same. Celebrating small wins helps you anchor yourself in the present and reinforces your belief in your own capacity. It keeps you engaged with your life—not just as a task, but as a playful adventure.

## The Deeper Why

Our brains are wired to notice what's missing, not what's working. It is a survival instinct that can quietly drain joy from everyday life. But when we pause to acknowledge even the tiniest progress, we interrupt that old pattern. Psychologically, celebrating small wins boosts dopamine, reinforces self-trust and gently rewires the brain to feel more capable and alive. It's not about pretending everything's perfect—it's about letting yourself feel proud, even in progress. That's the real fuel for playful, sustainable living.

## Try These Things

- Keep a "small wins" journal. At the end of each day, write down 2–3 things you feel good about—no matter how tiny.
- Create a "celebration playlist" and play one song every time you check something off your list.
- Make a ritual out of your celebrations—a happy dance, a self-hug, or a few words of appreciation for yourself.
- Share one small win with a friend every week. You'll be surprised at how validating it feels.

## Grounding Thoughts

You don't have to wait for the mountain to move. Celebrate the steps—dance for the one line written, the honest "no", the early bedtime and the scary "yes". These are not small things. These are sacred moments. When you honour them, life starts to feel a lot more like play—and a lot less like pressure.

# CHAPTER 12

# Playful Productivity— Getting Things Done Without Burning Out

There was a time when I thought productivity meant long hours and relentless effort. My to-do lists were overwhelming, and if I didn't tick every box, I'd feel like I had failed. It wasn't sustainable, and I was mentally and physically drained.

Then something shifted. I started experimenting with a different approach: *bringing play into the way I worked.* Instead of dragging myself through each task, I set up playful challenges—like writing a paragraph in ten minutes or seeing how quickly I could tidy my desk. I added music, movement and small rewards. I even made a game out of completing dull tasks. Slowly, work became something I looked forward to. The stress eased. I was still getting things done, sometimes even more than before, but with far more joy and creativity.

## Why Productivity Needs Play

Most of us grow up believing that being productive means being serious. Work hard, stay focused and push through; no time for anything light or fun. But this mindset can lead straight to burnout.

Play, on the other hand, naturally boosts *motivation, creativity and resilience*. Psychologists say that play activates the brain's reward systems, which helps us stay engaged and mentally flexible. Even adults need it—especially when we're overloaded.

When productivity feels playful:

- You stay motivated for longer
- You find creative ways to solve problems
- You avoid burnout
- You enjoy the process, not just the outcome

Whether you're a teacher planning lessons, a parent managing routines, or a manager navigating endless meetings, small doses of play can refresh your workflow and mindset.

## How to Bring Play into Your Work

- **Turn tasks into challenges**: Can you write that report faster than yesterday? Can you answer five emails before your coffee cools?
- **Use timers**: Try the Pomodoro method: 25 minutes of focused work, followed by a 5-minute break.
- **Add a layer of fun**: Put on music while you clean, brainstorm while you walking, or try colour-coding your to-do list like a puzzle.
- **Celebrate progress**: Even a tiny task deserves a little fist pump or a moment of celebration.

## Play in Action: What It Looks Like at Work and Home

- **Teacher:** Meera, a high school teacher, turns lesson reviews into quiz shows, complete with silly buzzers and team points. Her students actually *look forward* to revision.

- **Parent:** Ravi, a dad of two, sets a timer and makes cleaning a "race against the robot vacuum". The kids now beg to tidy up.
- **Corporate Professional:** Anjali, who works in HR, starts her team's weekly stand-ups with one-minute "absurd questions" (e.g., 'If our team were a snack, what would we be?'). It sounds silly—but it gets people laughing and relaxed before tackling tough tasks.
- **Freelancer:** Ritvik often sets a 25-minute timer and plays music he loves while writing — a practice he calls a "flow sprint." No checking his phone; just one task, one rhythm, one burst of joy.
- **Accountant:** Sashwat "plays with language" in small, practical ways that make his work more engaging. He explains complex concepts to clients in plain, vivid language — for instance, comparing profit margins to a "safety cushion" or describing cash flow as "the oxygen of a business." In reports or presentations, he turns dry data into short, meaningful stories that highlight progress or lessons learned. Even light touches — friendlier email subject lines, a hint of humor in team updates, or a personal record of "word wins" (phrases or analogies that worked well) — make his communication clearer and more enjoyable without losing professionalism.
- **Nurse:** For Neena, "playful mindfulness" means using small, in-the-moment techniques to stay centered without adding pressure. During a stressful shift, she takes mindful breaths while washing her hands or walking between patients, hums softly while restocking supplies, or shares quick, light-hearted moments with colleagues to release tension. Even brief observations — the feel of cool water, the steady beep of a monitor, or the warmth in a patient's thanks — bring her a quiet sense of awareness. It's not about being cheerful all the time, but about staying open, grounded, and gently human in the midst of intensity.

## The Deeper Why

Research shows that play boosts dopamine and can unlock a *flow state*—a zone of focus where you're fully immersed, energised and highly productive. In other words, play doesn't take away from your work—it helps you *get into it*.

But productivity without play often leads to pressure, not progress. Psychologically, when we work from a place of constant urgency or self-criticism, our nervous system shifts into *survival mode,* and creativity shuts down. But when we bring lightness, breaks and curiosity into the process, we tap into intrinsic motivation, not just willpower. That's the sweet spot: where we get things done not by pushing harder, but by working along the grain of our energy, not against it.

## Mini Pause: How Playful Is Your Productivity?

### Reflect on these:

- When do I feel most alive and focused at work?
- What's one small way I could bring fun into a routine task?
- Do I allow myself to enjoy the process—or only the results?

### Try the Productivity Play Challenge Card

Pick one of these each day this week and try it:

- Play your favourite upbeat song while working on a task you usually dread.
- Start your day by drawing your to-do list. Literally. Doodle it.
- Turn your next focus session into a game. Set a timer and "race" yourself to finish something before it goes off.
- Begin your next meeting or catch-up with a playful question, 'If today were a movie, what genre would it be?'

- Reward your progress with something fun—a dance break, a walk, or even a silly sticker.
- Try doing your most boring chore in the most dramatic way possible (opera voice encouraged).

## Reflect

- How does play change the way I feel about work?
- What gets in the way of letting work be fun?
- What can I do to keep this playful habit going?

## Grounding Thoughts

Play isn't just for children—it's fuel for sustainable work.

When you let work feel light, your energy returns, your creativity expands, and you get more done, without the burnout.

# CHAPTER 13
# "No" Is a Tiny Word with Superpowers

It all started when I got my puppy. She was this tiny ball of fluff, utterly dependent on me. Suddenly, I was up at 5:30 a.m. and sleeping by 10 p.m. My schedule was no longer mine—it belonged to her. Walks, meals, playtime, vet appointments, cleaning and cuddles felt like I was caring for a toddler.

For someone who had spent years being "always available" to people, this was a big change. Before the puppy, if a friend messaged at 10:30 p.m. wanting to chat, I'd respond. If someone needed help with their project, I'd say yes—even if I was exhausted. I was afraid of being "that person" who says no. I didn't want people to think I was selfish.

But soon, something shifted. The puppy forced me to say no to late-night calls, unnecessary errands and sometimes, even friends. At first, guilt gnawed at me. But as time passed, I started feeling something I hadn't felt in a long time—relief, freedom and joy.

I was finally saying yes to *myself.*

## Why Saying No Matters

Every time you say yes to someone out of guilt or fear, you're saying no to something else—often, your rest, your joy, your peace, or your creative spark.

Saying no isn't rejection; it's *redirection* of your time, your energy and your values. It's not about shutting people out; it's about letting yourself in.

We think of "no" as rude or abrupt. But, in truth, *no is a form of self-care.* It's your boundary wrapped in one syllable.

## Try The No Game

For the next week, practice saying no once a day. It can be small:

- No to extra sugar in your tea.
- No to watching a show just because everyone else is.
- No to picking up a call when you're not in the mood to talk.

Make it playful. Smile when you say it and let it feel light. Like a muscle, it gets stronger with use.

## The Deeper Why

Saying no isn't just a boundary—it's a psychological reset. It tells your nervous system that it's safe to protect your time, energy and truth. For many of us, especially if we've been conditioned to please or overextend, saying no feels risky. But every "no" is actually a "yes" to something more aligned.

Over time, these tiny choices rebuild self-trust, and that changes everything, because the most playful life isn't one filled with yeses, but one filled with clarity.

## A Few Ways to Say No (Without Feeling Guilty)

You don't always have to say "no" directly. Here are gentler alternatives:

- 'I'd love to, but I'm taking some time for myself right now.'

- 'That sounds great, but I already have plans to rest this evening.'
- 'I can't commit to this right now. Thanks for thinking of me!'
- 'Maybe another time. I'm recharging at the moment.'

Use language that's authentic to you. These phrases aren't excuses—they're boundaries set with grace.

## Reflect

- When was the last time you said yes when you really wanted to say no? Why?
- What would you gain if you started protecting your time more honestly?
- How would your creative life change if you honoured your own energy first?

## Stories That May Resonate

A friend of mine, a content creator in her early 20s, started saying no to late-night Zoom hangouts so she could journal and make art. She thought her online crew would feel rejected—but instead, they loved that she was setting boundaries and even started doing the same.

Another friend left a group chat that was constantly gossiping and draining. At first, she worried she'd miss out, but within a week, her anxiety dropped and she started filling that space with music and poetry again.

My cousin, Aarav, used to say yes to every group project, every club meeting and every side hustle. He thought hustle culture was the only way. But one day, he skipped a planning call and went skating instead. That small "no" reminded him that his worth isn't tied to how much he produces.

A college student I mentor always felt like the emotional first responder for her friends—always replying instantly to vent texts, even at 2 a.m. She finally sent a message saying, "I care, but I'm offline tonight to take care of my mental health." She was nervous, but her friends got it—and some even followed her lead.

A gamer and streamer I know used to take on every collab and stream session to "keep the momentum going", but burnout hit hard. Now, he says, 'Let me check my energy levels first,' before agreeing. Not only is he more present when he shows up, but his audience actually respects his vibe more now.

Saying "no" didn't make their lives smaller. It made them *richer*.

## Grounding Thoughts

You don't need a dramatic escape plan to protect your peace. Sometimes, all it takes is a one-syllable spell. It's not rude or selfish, it's how you guard your energy, your time and your joy.

In fact, saying "no' is not just an act of courage, but also an act of kindness to yourself. When you say no to what drains you, you say yes to what fills you.

No isn't rejection—it's a superpower. Use it wisely.

# CHAPTER 14

# Playful Mindfulness—Being Present Without Pressure

Chapter 14: Playful Mindfulness—Being Present Without Pressure

I remember one afternoon sitting on my terrace with a cup of tea. There was no checklist, no big goal for the day—just a sense of quiet. I started to observe the little things: a crow cawing from the overhead wire, the swirls of steam rising from my cup, even the warmth of the sun on my knees. I wasn't "trying" to be mindful. In fact, I had no plan to meditate or reflect that day.

But in those moments, I felt completely present. I wasn't judging myself for not being productive; I wasn't pushing myself to "feel" anything. I just *was*. It felt like my mind was a child playing in a field—free, curious and completely absorbed in the now.

That was the day I truly understood what it meant to be mindful without making it a task. It was playful, natural and pressure-free.

## What Is Playful Mindfulness?

Mindfulness sounds serious, right? Like sitting still for hours, clearing your mind, chasing enlightenment. But let's flip that. Mindfulness can be playful, easy and alive—a way to show up for your life without the pressure to "do it right". It's noticing without judging or getting overly attached to the situation, being curious about your moment-to-moment experience and choosing to enjoy the ride—even the bumps.

It's not about perfection, it's about presence, with a wink.

## How to Practice Without Stress

- It's not always easy, but see if you can, notice your breath—like watching a kite sway, sometimes smooth, sometimes restless.
- Take a playful pause—smell your coffee, listen to birds, feel the sun on your skin.
- When your mind wanders, imagine it like a puppy chasing butterflies—gentle, kind and always ready to come back.

One day, I was brushing my teeth and caught myself going over an imaginary argument in my head. Then I noticed the coolness of the water, the sound of the bristles and the tiny bubbles. I chuckled. Here I was, in my own bathroom, creating drama in my mind while minty foam danced on my lips. I slowed down and just brushed—and strangely, I felt calmer, more real. That's playful mindfulness in action. Nothing grand. Just waking up to what's already here.

## Mini Pause: Your Mindfulness Playground

Ask yourself:

- When do I feel most present?
- What small moments can I savour today?
- How can I think curiously instead of having judgemental thoughts?

## Try These Mindful Moments

- Pick one everyday activity (brushing teeth, walking, eating) and do it slowly, noticing every detail.

- Set a reminder to pause and take three deep breaths, smiling each time.
- Use playful mental images or metaphors to gently guide your focus.

## Reflect

- How does playful mindfulness change how I experience my day?
- What's easier or harder about being present this way?
- Which moments invite my attention naturally?
- What does it feel like when presence comes without pressure?

## Reminder

Mindfulness isn't a task. It's a playful dance with your experience—lighthearted, alive and always available.

# CHAPTER 15

# Bringing It All Together—Your Playful Life Blueprint

You've come a long way.

Through reflection, play, creativity and courage, you've explored parts of yourself that maybe you hadn't visited in a while. Maybe you've danced a little, maybe you've cried. Maybe you've had quiet revelations or unexpected giggles. Whatever your journey through this book looked like, I want you to know that it matters.

Now it's time to gather the pieces, honour the shifts and create your very own *Playful Life Blueprint.*

This isn't a rigid plan. It's a flexible, soulful reminder of what makes you feel alive. A playful life doesn't follow rules—it listens, adjusts and responds with love. Your blueprint is yours to shape, evolve and carry forward.

Let me share mine with you first.

My personal blueprint includes:

- Writing stories and songs that come from my own heart
- Dancing like a total goofball when no one's watching
- Letting music guide my emotions
- Going out with friends and saying "yes" to life more often
- Creating space for silence and spontaneity
- Remembering to breathe, even when I feel like everything's too much

## Your Playful Life Blueprint

This one's for you! Here's a simple way to bring all the ideas from this book together into a joyful rhythm. Think of this not as a rigid plan, but as a flexible invitation—a way to return to your playful self whenever you feel lost, tired, or disconnected.

1. Energy Anchors
   List 3–5 things that energise you—music, a walk, laughter with a friend, or even just making art. These are your go-to sources when you need a reset.

2. Playful Rituals
   Identify one small, regular activity that brings joy—watering a plant, flipping through a favorite book, or taking a short walk to feel the sun on your face.

3. Micro-Wins Celebration
   Note ways you can celebrate small acts—a post-it note with a "You did it!", clapping for yourself after sending a tough email, or taking a victory sip of chai after a tricky conversation.

4. Joyful "Nos"
   List three situations or behaviours you often say yes to out of guilt, and rewrite them with a confident no.
   *(Eg: No to social plans when I'm exhausted = yes to rest.)*

5. Flow Zones
   Identify the time of day, kind of space, or activity where you feel most immersed or at ease. These are your creative zones—protect them.

6. Connection Without Exhaustion
   Think of people or groups that energise you. Make a note of ways to connect more intentionally without feeling drained.

Bonus: A detailed version of this is available in the "Play Lab" section towards the end of the book. You can fill it in right then and there or download and print a one-page version of this blueprint, too. Fill it out and pin it where you'll see it often. Let it evolve with you.

## Extra Garnish: Key Ingredients in a Playful Life

You can create your own blueprint, too! Here are some ingredients you might want to include in it. Take what resonates and leave what doesn't.

1. **Curiosity** A playful life begins with wondering, "What if?" or "Why not?" Let your questions guide you.
2. **Compassion** Play thrives when there's room to be messy and imperfect. Have compassion towards yourself and others.
3. **Creativity** Not for productivity, but for joy. Paint, doodle, hum, cook, garden—whatever makes your soul sigh in relief.
4. **Connection** With nature, with people and with your own spirit. Play often shows up in the in-between spaces.
5. **Courage** Be seen, fail and try again. Play asks for brave softness.
6. **Rest** Yes, rest. A playful life needs room to breathe. Doing nothing is sacred.

## A Living, Breathing Blueprint

Remember—your blueprint isn't a final destination. It's a compass that shifts with your seasons. What brings you joy today may look different a year from now. That's not a failure; it's growth. You get to revisit, revise and reimagine your playful life whenever you need to.

If you'd like, there are bonus blueprint worksheets and a toolkit with references to books and podcasts to incorporate more play into your life—you'll find it at the end of the book inside the Play Lab.

## Woo-hoo! You made it to the End!

Dear Reader,

If you've made it this far, let me first say—thank you. Thank you for showing up, for not just these pages, but for yourself. This book isn't just something I wrote; it's something I lived, stumbled through, laughed with, cried alongside and eventually grew with. Writing it was like tracing the map of my own playful life, and now, here you are, unfolding that map and making it your own.

When I first began thinking about play, I realised how often we treat it like a reward—something we can have *after* everything else is done. But what if play was not the dessert but the nourishment? What if it's what brings us back to life, again and again?

My playful blueprint is still evolving. Some days it's a messy song I record on my phone, some days it's dancing barefoot while cooking dinner. And on other days, it's doing absolutely nothing, and feeling joy in the nothingness. I don't always get it right. But I've learned to return to play when I'm lost, tired, or unsure.

I hope this book has helped you reconnect with your inner spark—the one that knows how to wonder, giggle, scribble, sing, explore and feel wildly, unapologetically *you*.

I appreciate you walking this journey with me. For every reflection, every laugh, every moment you choose to stay with yourself instead of drifting away—you've honoured your own life force.

If you're wondering what comes next, there's a little something waiting for you in the *Play Lab* section—an open invitation, not homework. So, go take a look!

Also, if you'd like to share your experience, ask questions, or simply say hello, you can reach me at *divya.ovya@gmail.com*. I'd love to hear from you.

This isn't goodbye. This is your beginning. I'm cheering you on from wherever I am.

You're doing beautifully. Keep playing.

With so much love and play,
*Divya*

## What Next? Play Lab Activity Set

You've read this book. You've explored what play means, why it matters and how it shows up in creativity, connection and care. But this book isn't meant to be a one-time read. It's a blueprint—a gentle guide to help you rediscover something you already have inside you: *your own playful state.*

## Knowing About Play isn't the same as Living It.

That's where this final section comes in.

What follows is an *invitation*—ten light, joyful, sometimes mischievous ways to *experience* what we've talked about.

The idea is to break the monotony by approaching everyday activities in more creative and playful ways. This allows your mind to engage with different parts of itself, opening up new perspectives and fresh energy. By shifting how you experience the routine, you invite deeper exploration and a richer connection to your creativity.

These aren't rigid exercises; they're playful experiments.

Try them.

Break them.

Make your own versions.

Do them with a friend or in secret. The point isn't to do them right—it's just to *do them with delight.*

*Welcome to the Play Lab.*

## Your Playful Life Blueprint

*A gentle, joyful guide to reconnect with your energy, creativity and playfulness.*

1. **Energy Anchors**
What lifts your spirit when you feel low or stuck?

List *3–5 activities* or *people* that never fail to recharge you.

### Examples:

- Singing to a favourite playlist
- Walking barefoot on grass
- Laughing with a certain friend
- Doodling or painting freely

**Your Turn:** What are 5 things that energise you—physically, emotionally, or creatively?

1. _____
2. _____
3. _____
4. _____
5. _____

### Bonus Prompt:

What's one small way you can *add* more of these into your week?

## 2. **Playful Rituals**

*Tiny acts. Daily joy.*

List or describe *one small ritual* that feels like your personal spark.

## Examples:

- Writing a kind note to yourself
- Playing a favorite song
- Savoring a square of chocolate

**Your Turn:** What's one current ritual that feels playful or comforting?

What's one new one you'd like to try?

My current ritual:

_____

One I'd love to try:

_____

## Optional Reflection:

How do you feel *before and after* doing this ritual?

_____

_____

## 3. **Micro-Wins Celebration**

Why wait for big milestones? Celebrate tiny victories.

## Examples:

- "I replied to that message I was dreading. High-five!"
- "I cooked today even though I was tired. Gold star."
- "I chose rest instead of people-pleasing. Yes!"

**Your Turn:** List 3 tiny wins from *this past week* and how you can celebrate them.

| Win | Celebration |
|---|---|
| _____ | _____ |
| _____ | _____ |
| _____ | _____ |

What's your signature victory move? (e.g., chai toast, a little dance, a sticky note on the fridge):

_____

_____

### 4. Joyful "Nos"

Every *no* is a *yes* to yourself.

## Examples:

- "No to last-minute favours = Yes to my peace"
- "No to explaining myself = Yes to self-trust"

**Your Turn:** Think of 3 things you often say yes to out of guilt or habit. Rewrite them with a clear and joyful *"no"*.

| Old Habitual Yes | Joyful No & What It Makes Space For |
|---|---|
| _____ | _____ |
| _____ | _____ |
| _____ | _____ |

### 5. Flow Zones

Where does time dissolve and energy rise?

**Reflect:** When during the day do I feel most focused and alive? What space or activity makes me lose track of time?

## Examples:

- Early mornings by the window with tea
- Working on a creative task with lo-fi music
- Journaling in a quiet café

## Your Flow Zone Map:

Time of day: _____

Place or setting: _____

Activity or type of task: _____

How can I set aside at least 30 minutes, a few times a week, to be in this zone?

_____

### 6. Connection Without Exhaustion
Relationships that fill you up, not wear you down.

**Prompt:** Who makes me feel seen, safe, or silly in the best way? How can I connect with them more intentionally (without pressure)?

| **Person/Group** | **Energising Way to Connect** |
|---|---|
| _____ | _____ |
| _____ | _____ |
| _____ | _____ |

**Boundary Reminder:** What's one draining interaction I want to *limit*—and how might I do that kindly?

# WORKSHEET 1

# Relearning What Play Feels Like

**Mini Insight:** We often confuse play with an activity, but play is something that puts you into a *state of being*. Play feels light, curious, free and unpressured. This worksheet helps you identify your personal "playful state".

## Try This:

- Think of a moment you felt *joyfully absorbed*—not for a goal, but just because it felt good. Write it down.
- Now answer:
    - What were you doing?
    - Who were you with (or were you alone)?
    - How did time feel?
    - What sensations or emotions came up?

**Reflect:** What makes you lose track of time and feel like a kid again?

# WORKSHEET 2

# The "What If This Were a Game?" Trick

**Mini Insight:** Play doesn't need new activities. It needs a new lens. Ask: *What if this were a game?*

## Try This:

Choose a boring or frustrating task you do often, like folding laundry or replying to emails. Turn it into a game:

- Add a challenge ("Can I do this with only 5 clicks?")
- Add a reward
- Add a silly rule ("I sing every third word")

**Reflect:** Did the task feel lighter? Why or why not?

# WORKSHEET 3

# Invite Your Inner Mischief

**Mini Insight:** Playfulness is often mischievous—it bends rules gently, surprises you and adds *quirkiness* to your life.

## Try This:

- Write three small quirky and fun acts you can do today. (Examples: Wear mismatched socks, speak in rhyme for five minutes, give objects new names)
- Try one.

**Reflect:** How did it feel to break the rhythm?

# WORKSHEET 4

# Play with Senses

**Mini Insight:** One fast way to enter play is through the *senses* — colour, texture, sound, taste. It brings you into the now.

## Try This:

- Take 15 minutes and explore one sense like a curious child.
    - *Touch:* Feel different fabrics in your room
    - *Sight:* Create an outfit using three bold colours
    - *Sound:* Make a 1-minute beat using your desk
    - *Taste:* Mix a funny drink from the items in your kitchen

**Reflect:** What did you notice when you gave yourself permission to explore?

# WORKSHEET 5

# Let Go of the Outcome

**Mini Insight:** Play isn't about the result; it's about the process. Try making or doing something new. Even if it turns out bad, love it anyway.

## Try This:

- Draw a portrait of yourself
- Write a 5-line poem with made-up words
- Walk backwards for a few minutes or do activities with your non-dominant hand

**Reflect:** What was it like to *not care* how it turned out?

# WORKSHEET 6

# Build a Character for a Day

**Mini Insight:** Kids roleplay all the time. Adults can do it too, through outfits, accents and mannerisms. It's a route to freedom.

**Try This:**

- Create a playful persona: name, hobby, secret power and so on
- Be them for 30 minutes—in speech, posture, outfits and all

**Reflect:** What part of you came alive in that character?

# 7 WORKSHEET

# Add a Surprise to Routine

**Mini Insight:** Routine dulls play, but *spontaneity* sparks it. A playful life makes room for the unexpected.

## Try This:

- Plan one twist in your day—take a different route, eat dessert first, or write a note to a stranger
- Let spontaneity in

**Reflect:** How did it affect your energy or mood?

# 8 WORKSHEET | Invite Someone to Play

**Mini Insight:** Play is contagious. Sometimes we just need one more person to say "yes" to unleash it.

## Try This:

- Invite a friend to do something silly, short, or strange with you (even just ten minutes counts)
- Examples: Make a collage, invent a handshake, play charades with random objects, etc

**Reflect:** How did shared play feel different from solo play?

# WORKSHEET 9

# Design a 10-Minute Play Break

**Mini Insight:** You don't need a full day to feel playful. You need *intention and permission*.

## Try This:

- Create a menu of five playful mini-breaks you can take during a dull workday
- Examples: Bubble wrap popping, scribble and rip, kitchen beatboxing, or doodle race with a timer

**Reflect:** Which one felt the most energising?

# 10 WORKSHEET | Your Play Philosophy

**Mini Insight:** Play isn't a luxury—it's a way of life. What kind of play-filled life are you building?

**Try This:**

Complete these:

- "I know I am in a playful state when I feel _____."
- "I want more play in my life because _____."
- "I give myself permission to play even when _____."

**Reflect:** What would your week look like if you prioritised joy over performance?

# The Playful Living Toolkit

Books, podcasts and tools to inspire more joy, flow and creativity.

## Books

- *Big Magic* by Elizabeth Gilbert - On creativity, courage and the magic of doing what you love without fear.
- *The Art of Noticing* by Rob Walker - A collection of prompts to help you slow down and rediscover wonder in the everyday.
- *Play* by Stuart Brown, MD - A scientific and personal exploration of how play shapes our brains, relationships and lives.
- *The Gifts of Imperfection* by Brené Brown - Encouragement to embrace authenticity and let go of perfectionism.
- *The Artist's Way* by Julia Cameron - A classic guide for unlocking creative flow, filled with exercises and reflection prompts.

## Podcasts

- *Unlocking Us* by Brené Brown - Conversations about vulnerability, connection and wholehearted living.
- *Creative Pep Talk* by Andy J Pizza - Bursting with inspiration, humour and helpful insights for artists and dreamers.
- *On Being* with Krista Tippett - Soulful dialogues on meaning, mindfulness and what it means to be alive.
- *The Long and The Short Of It* by Jen Waldman and Peter Shepherd - Smart, light-hearted takes on living intentionally and creatively.

## Apps and Tools

- *Headspace* or *Insight Timer* - For calming and accessible guided meditations.
- *One Second Everyday* - Helps document small joys by recording a one-second video each day.
- *Notion* or *Journey* - Digital tools for journalling, organising and building your playful life blueprint.
- *Coffitivity* - An ambient sound app to spark creativity with café-style background noise.
- *Habitica* - A gamified habit tracker that helps you turn personal goals into small, rewarding quests.

# Note of Gratitude

Writing this book has been a journey of discovery, play and growth. I want to thank everyone who inspired and supported me along the way.

To my family and friends, thank you for your endless encouragement and for believing in my vision, even when I doubted myself.

To Harshita, who read the book deeply, dissected its essence and gave me honest, generous feedback that made the book sharper, clearer and more grounded.

To Ram and Sunit, who reminded me that not everyone reads a book cover to cover. They helped me understand how it could work for non-bookish readers, too—and how skimming, pausing, or flipping through is valid, even playful, in itself.

To Kriti, my collaborator in many art workshops, who always spoke about the beauty of *breaking the flow*, changing direction midway, disrupting patterns and finding something unexpected through that chaos. Watching her work taught me that this mindset doesn't just lead to interesting art, but to a more gamified, curious and lively life.

And to Bala and Arjun, who introduced me to the world of improv—and showed me how playfulness isn't something you *visit*, but something you can *live*. With them, I learned that presence, responsiveness and lightness can be almost religiously ingrained in every moment of life.

To Rohit, who has this quiet superpower of making even my heaviest thoughts feel a little more *playful and light*. His way of seeing the world—with humour, perspective and ease—reminded me that play can live in the way we speak, think and connect.

To Perry, the heart behind Urban Solace, who inspires me to keep sharing my work and offers a platform where creativity and community can bloom. His consistency and generosity in creating space for artists to engage are truly amazing.

To Kalpesh, my art mentor, who showed me that there is no end to constant improvement and learning, a reminder that every step forward is part of the playful journey itself.

To Lagori Labs and Siddharth, who opened my eyes to the power of imaginative storytelling through gamification, showing how narrative and play can weave together to create deeper engagement and joy.

To Apoorvalakshmi, founder of MultipotX—a vibrant hub for multipassionates. Apoorva helped me realise that I am not alone in embracing multidimensional interests, and that there is a whole community of beautiful, curious souls like me.

To Jaaga Creative Bangalore, for showing me how playful, meaningful engagement can thrive online. Their workshops were a masterclass in creating worldwide connection and joy through digital spaces, delivered with a unique finesse that truly inspired me.

To my creative tribe—the artists, musicians, writers and kindred spirits—your energy and collaboration have fueled my passion and kept my spirit alive.

To my mentors, who showed me the power of mindfulness, presence and taking up space authentically, your guidance has been invaluable.

And finally, to my dog Bella, who constantly teaches me what it means to be fully in the moment—to notice, to breathe, to just *be*.

And to you, dear reader, thank you for choosing to explore this playful path with me. May this book inspire you to embrace your unique self and live life with joyful intention.

## IndiePress

The best route your story can take.

To publish your own book, contact us.

We publish poetry collections, short story collections, novellas and novels.

contact@http://indiepress.in/

Instagram- indie_press